HABITAT
PRESERVATION

Andrew J. Milson, Ph.D.
Content Consultant
University of Texas at Arlington

Acknowledgments

Grateful acknowledgment is given to the authors, artists, photographers, museums, publishers, and agents for permission to reprint copyrighted material. Every effort has been made to secure the appropriate permission. If any omissions have been made or if corrections are required, please contact the Publisher.

Instructional Consultant: Christopher Johnson, Evanston, Illinois

Teacher Reviewer: Julie Mitchell, Lake Forest Middle School, Cleveland, Tennessee

Photographic Credits
Front Cover, Inside Front Cover, Title Page
©Chris Newbert/Minden Pictures. **4** (bg) ©imago stock&people/Newscom. **6** (bg) ©Jacques Jangoux/ Photo Researchers/Getty Images. **7** (bl) ©Carl Purcell/Carl & Ann Purcell/Corbis. **8** (bg) Mapping Specialists. **10** (bg) ©Winfried Schäfer/imagebroker/ agefotostock. **11** (tl) ©Nigel Pavitt/JAI/Corbis. **12** (t) ©Albert Moldvay/National Geographic Stock. **13** (t) ©Chris Hellier/Corbis. **14** (bg) ©Philip Dumas/ Flickr Unreleased/Getty Images. **16** (bg) ©Brand X Pictures/Jupiterimages. **18** (t) ©Wolfgang Kaehler/ Corbis. **20** (bl) ©Gerald & Buff Corsi/Visuals Unlimited/Corbis. (bg) ©Kent Kobersteen/National Geographic Society/Corbis. **22** (bg) ©Tom Brakefield/ Corbis. **23** (tl) ©Beverly Joubert/National Geographic Stock. **24** (bg) ©Beverly Joubert/National Geographic Stock. **27** (t) ©AP Photo/John David Mercer. **28** (tr) ©LeoFFreitas/Flickr/Getty Images. **30** (tc) ©imago stock&people/Newscom. (bl) ©Gerald & Buff Corsi/Visuals Unlimited/Corbis. **31** (bg) ©PhotoDisc/Getty Images. (tr) ©John Foxx Images/Imagestate. (br) ©Chris Hellier/Corbis. (br) ©Peter Solness/Lonely Planet Images/Getty Images.

MetaMetrics® and the MetaMetrics logo and tagline are trademarks of MetaMetrics, Inc., and are registered in the United States and abroad. The trademarks and names of other companies and products mentioned herein are the property of their respective owners. Copyright © 2010 MetaMetrics, Inc. All rights reserved.

For permission to use material from this text or product, submit all requests online at www.cengage.com/permissions

Further permissions questions can be emailed to permissionrequest@cengage.com

Visit National Geographic Learning online at www.NGSP.com.

Visit our corporate website at www.cengage.com.

Printed in the USA.

RR Donnelley, Menasha, WI

ISBN: 978-07362-97776

14 15 16 17 18 19 20 21 22

10 9 8 7 6 5 4 3

SAVING
Habitat

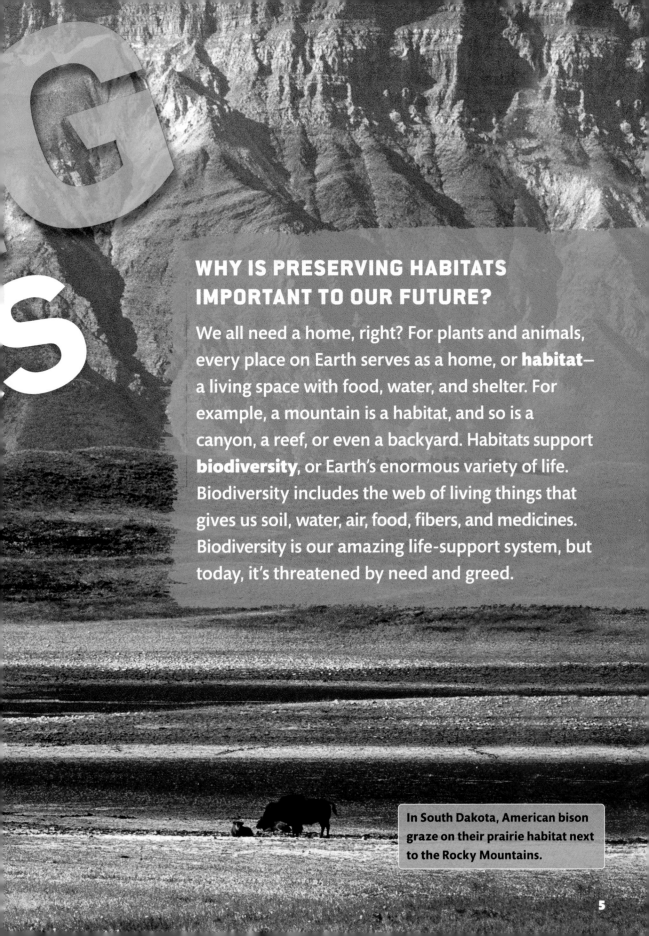

WHY IS PRESERVING HABITATS IMPORTANT TO OUR FUTURE?

We all need a home, right? For plants and animals, every place on Earth serves as a home, or **habitat**—a living space with food, water, and shelter. For example, a mountain is a habitat, and so is a canyon, a reef, or even a backyard. Habitats support **biodiversity**, or Earth's enormous variety of life. Biodiversity includes the web of living things that gives us soil, water, air, food, fibers, and medicines. Biodiversity is our amazing life-support system, but today, it's threatened by need and greed.

In South Dakota, American bison graze on their prairie habitat next to the Rocky Mountains.

THREATS CLOSE TO HOME

In 2011, Earth's human population topped 7 billion, spiking the global demand for land, water, and other resources. Sheer numbers of people are damaging many habitats and the **species**, or kinds of living things, that need them. When habitats disappear, species die and biodiversity suffers.

Globally, agriculture is one major cause of habitat loss. Most of the world's poorest 1 billion people are farmers who take over forests and grazing lands as they need more land and energy. Removing trees in an area of forest to convert the land for farming or other uses is called **deforestation**. Pesticides and fertilizers cause further damage.

Urban sprawl—the spread of cities into surrounding land—also eats up pastures, wetlands, and forests. Each day in the United States, 6,000 acres of land are consumed by housing, factories, and malls—an area as big as 4,500 football fields!

This method of deforestation in Brazil is called slash-and-burn. Farmers commonly use this method to get more land for planting.

GLOBAL WORRIES

Wealthy and developing countries devour five to ten times more resources than the poorest countries. The actions of affluent countries affect the entire planet. Wealthy countries burn the most fossil fuels, which warm the atmosphere, and they consume most of the world's lands, forests, minerals, and fisheries. They also churn out most of the world's garbage, industrial wastes, and other pollutants. This **overconsumption** uses resources faster than nature can replace them.

In the last 30 years, people have exhausted one-third of Earth's resources, destroying habitats too quickly for many species to adjust. If this population growth and consumption continue, we'll need 1.5 planet Earths to keep up! The United Nations (UN) estimates that every day, 150–200 species become **extinct**, or disappear forever. According to the UN, the world is now facing the largest mass extinction since 65 million years ago, when the dinosaurs disappeared.

Conservation is the vital work of preserving habitats and living things. Many conservationists, people who participate in conservation efforts, turn out to be ordinary people. In the following pages you will read about problems in Madagascar and Antarctica. In these areas, ordinary people came together to solve them.

In the Florida Everglades, habitat destruction has reduced the marsh area to half its former size due to agriculture, urban sprawl, runoff pollution, and loss of water resources.

Explore the Issue

1. **Identify Problems** What are some major causes of habitat destruction?

2. **Analyze Cause and Effect** How do booming populations and overconsumption affect habitats and biodiversity?

Habitats in

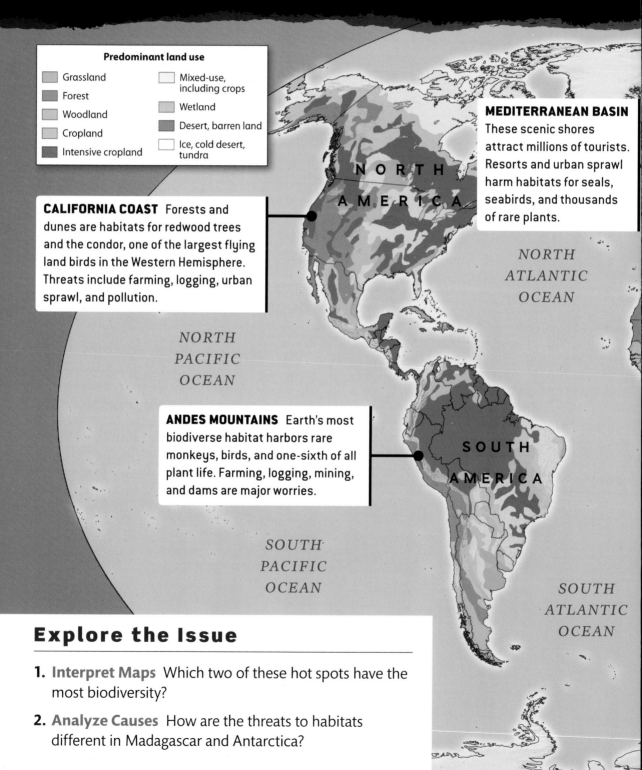

Predominant land use

- Grassland
- Forest
- Woodland
- Cropland
- Intensive cropland
- Mixed-use, including crops
- Wetland
- Desert, barren land
- Ice, cold desert, tundra

MEDITERRANEAN BASIN These scenic shores attract millions of tourists. Resorts and urban sprawl harm habitats for seals, seabirds, and thousands of rare plants.

CALIFORNIA COAST Forests and dunes are habitats for redwood trees and the condor, one of the largest flying land birds in the Western Hemisphere. Threats include farming, logging, urban sprawl, and pollution.

ANDES MOUNTAINS Earth's most biodiverse habitat harbors rare monkeys, birds, and one-sixth of all plant life. Farming, logging, mining, and dams are major worries.

NORTH AMERICA

SOUTH AMERICA

NORTH ATLANTIC OCEAN

NORTH PACIFIC OCEAN

SOUTH PACIFIC OCEAN

SOUTH ATLANTIC OCEAN

Explore the Issue

1. **Interpret Maps** Which two of these hot spots have the most biodiversity?

2. **Analyze Causes** How are the threats to habitats different in Madagascar and Antarctica?

Danger

Study the map below to learn about threatened habitats, many with species found nowhere else.

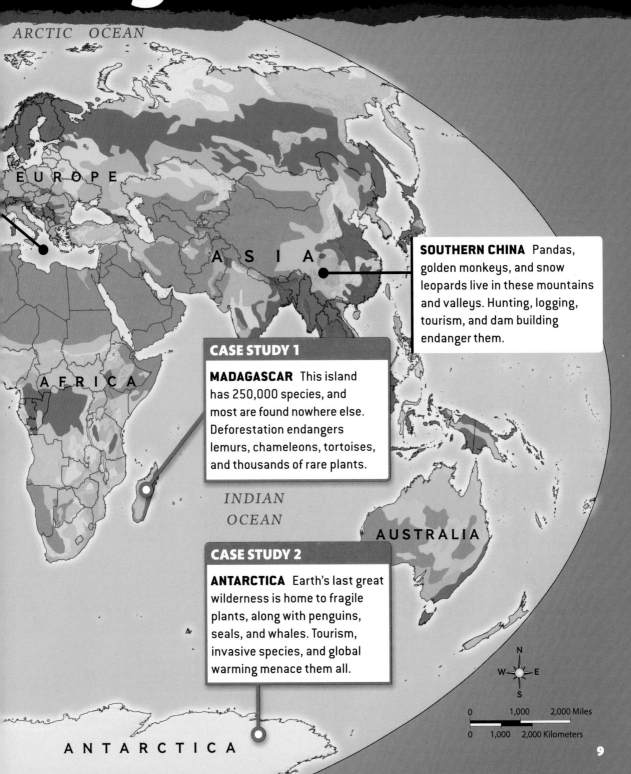

ARCTIC OCEAN

EUROPE

ASIA

AFRICA

SOUTHERN CHINA Pandas, golden monkeys, and snow leopards live in these mountains and valleys. Hunting, logging, tourism, and dam building endanger them.

CASE STUDY 1

MADAGASCAR This island has 250,000 species, and most are found nowhere else. Deforestation endangers lemurs, chameleons, tortoises, and thousands of rare plants.

INDIAN OCEAN

AUSTRALIA

CASE STUDY 2

ANTARCTICA Earth's last great wilderness is home to fragile plants, along with penguins, seals, and whales. Tourism, invasive species, and global warming menace them all.

ANTARCTICA

N
W E
S

0   1,000   2,000 Miles
0   1,000   2,000 Kilometers

The indri, the largest living lemur, has only one habitat: Madagascar. The indri travels exclusively through trees, jumping vertically from trunk to trunk.

Saving MADAGASCA SPECIES

A MAMMAL THAT FLIES

"Come quickly!" Marie Razafindrasolo (raz-zuh-fin-druh-SOH-loh) calls to tourists in the Madagascar (mad-duh-GASS-sker) rain forest. High in the canopy of treetops, a black and white indri springs off a limb, flies 30 feet through the air, and grabs a distant tree. Tourists snap photographs as fast as they can.

The tree-dwelling indri is the biggest of all lemurs, mammals called **primates** that include monkeys, apes, and humans. In the local language, "indri" means "Look up!" This striking lemur resembles "a four-year-old child in a panda suit equipped with an eerie territorial cry that is part aria and part air-raid siren," one observer declared.

This panther chameleon has eyes that rotate independently of each other; it can see 360 degrees around itself.

After the indri bounds away, Marie amazes the tourists with more unique sights. They see lizards masquerading as leaves and panther chameleons with rotating eyes. Marie enjoys her work. She and many others found new careers with the Andasibe Guides Association. It started more than 10 years ago to help people and to save forests.

MADE IN MADAGASCAR

The fourth largest island in the world, Madagascar sits 250 miles off the southeastern coast of Africa. It's been isolated for 80 million years, an extraordinary wonderland of life.

Scientists estimate that 250,000 species thrive in Madagascar, making it one of Earth's most biodiverse places. About 90 percent of Madagascar's plants and 70 percent of its animals live nowhere else. Western dry forests support lemurs, rare tortoises, and baobabs—strange bottle-shaped trees. Eastern rain forests also nurture lemurs, along with twig snakes, tomato-colored frogs, and spiders whose webs are 80 feet wide!

With so many species crammed into such a small space, even the tiniest habitats are crucial. For example, the mouse lemur weighs one ounce, and it consumes a sugary "honeydew," an excretion of a white bug that feeds on one species of vine in one patch of forest. If that patch is destroyed, the vine, the bug, the lemur, and many more species will be driven to extinction.

Before slash-and-burn farming, this field of baobab trees on the left is healthy. After the slashing and burning, the field on the right is devastated.

CUTTING FORESTS TO LIVE

Losing patches of trees—even whole forests—is a huge crisis in Madagascar. More than 90 percent of its forests have been cut down, and each year, people destroy enough trees to cover more than 12,000 city blocks. This rampant deforestation is the main cause of habitat loss and extinctions.

Madagascar's growing human population of 22 million is a primary cause of deforestation. More than 77 percent of Malagasy people live on less than $1 a day, and many practice **slash-and-burn agriculture**. This farming method involves cutting areas of forest to open up land for crops and then burning off the debris and leaving ashes to fertilize the soil. After a few years of planting, the soil loses the nutrients that allow it to support crops, and the cycle commences yet again.

Scrubby plants and grasses take over the abandoned fields. This vegetation doesn't grip the red earth as well as trees, so every year, rains erode 1,000 tons of soil per acre. From the air, rivers swollen with red soil make Madagascar look as if it's bleeding.

TIMBER THIEVES

Loggers are also illegally destroying swaths of rain forest, even in national parks. Criminal gangs hire farmers to cut rosewood and ebony trees, which are some of the rarest and most valuable species. These exotic trees are used to make costly guitars and furniture, like the million-dollar rosewood beds popular in Asia.

In a poor country like Madagascar, harvesting trees—even illegally—provides income. Cutting trees pays $5 a day. Dragging a log from the forest pays $10 to $20 per tree, substantial money for hungry families. Men who float the logs downriver earn $25 per tree. Some park rangers take $200 bribes to look away and let the criminals steal the trees.

Madagascar's government fell under a military coup in 2009, and during the chaos, thieves stole about 100,000 trees. Also, hunters seized chameleons and tortoises for the pet trade and killed lemurs for their meat, which they sold to Madagascar's city restaurants.

Reducing poverty is important so that people no longer have to rely on harmful practices.

This tree nursery, run by the Association Mitsinjo reserve, grows seedlings to restore the forest corridors destroyed by slash-and-burn agriculture. Less than 10 percent of Madagascar's original forest is left.

SEEDLINGS TAKE ROOT

Conservationists realize that to protect the forests, they must also help the people of Madagascar fight their way out of poverty. Reducing poverty is important so that people no longer have to rely on harmful practices. In 2011, for example, the World Bank allocated $52 million to protect 30 national parks and improve the lives of 90,000 Malagasy families.

Conservation efforts are also creating jobs in Madagascar. At Andasibe-Mantadia National Park, local people are restoring a rain forest ruined by logging. Workers collect seeds from about 120 species of trees and then raise 100,000 seedlings a year in five nurseries. When the saplings are strong, the men plant them in leafy corridors that link fragments of forest, thus giving wildlife safe passage to larger habitats. Lemurs need at least 2,500 acres to roam, so the corridors greatly enlarge their range. By 2011, one million saplings had taken root.

TOURISTS BRING HOPE

More than half of the 250,000-plus travelers who visit Madagascar are nature-loving ecotourists. Their presence furnishes jobs for local people in hotels and restaurants. Tourist money supports reforestation, modernized farming, and other conservation projects. Local guides and their communities share half of all national park fees paid by tourists.

Association Mitsinjo benefits directly from nature-based tourism. Its guides can handle many languages as well as scientific data about habitats and species. The staff at Mitsinjo are experts on indri, and they now assist scientists from abroad.

These efforts spell hope. Many locals, such as farmer Claude, want to save the forests. Claude admits, "I'm like the people who live here, we used the forest the same way, for slash-and-burn agriculture. But when I see the wrong destruction, I change my mind. I have the mind of a conservationist."

Explore the Issue

1. **Identify Causes** What are the causes of continuing deforestation in Madagascar?

2. **Analyze Solutions** Why does improving the lives of Malagasy people help to protect the country's habitats?

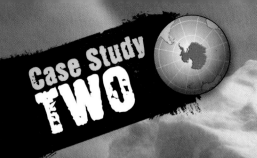

Tourists Threaten
ANTARCT

This iceberg lies in the Lamaire Channel, a top cruise destination for tourists to Antarctica. Those tourists are endangering the continent's habitat.

A RUDE AWAKENING

B-A-N-G! . . . . In the middle of a still November night in 2007, the cruise ship M/S *Explorer* was crunching through ice near Antarctica when suddenly it struck an iceberg. Water began pouring from toilets, alarms wailed, and terrified passengers raced from their cabins.

All 154 people on board scrambled into lifeboats and escaped from the ship. Near dawn, the shivering travelers were pulled to safety by two cruise ships sailing nearby.

These tourists were incredibly lucky. Antarctica is a remote, frozen wilderness with no cities, hospitals, or rescuers—just 45 scattered research stations. Fortunately, on that night, waters were calm and assistance was just 40 miles away.

The M/S *Explorer* sank later that day, the first tourist ship to be lost in these waters. Its sinking raised an important question: "How should Antarctic tourism be controlled?"

THE GREAT WHITE CONTINENT

Antarctica is the coldest, windiest, and driest continent on Earth. It's enormous, too—one and a half times the size of the United States. A vast sheet of ice, miles thick, covers 98 percent of the land and holds 70 percent of Earth's freshwater. Yet Antarctica is a desert. In fact, it's one of the world's largest deserts. Antarctica gets only 8 inches of precipitation a year because its frigid air is too cold to hold water vapor. Only plants such as lichens and moss, small insects and worms, and breeding birds and seals are adapted to this icy land.

On the other hand, many species thrive in the mild climate of the Antarctic Peninsula, which stretches 1,200 miles toward South America. This **peninsula**, a strip of land jutting out from the mainland, and nearby islands support more species. The surrounding food-rich oceans teem with whales, seals, penguins, and flying seabirds well suited to the frigid temperatures. Many of these species have layers of insulating fat, and oily feathers waterproof the penguins. Most fish even have an antifreeze-like substance in their bodies.

Antarctica might seem like an icy wasteland, but it helps control the global climate and holds many keys to understanding climate change. It is also Earth's last great wilderness.

THE TOURIST BOOM

Antarctic tourism took off in 1969 when explorer Lars-Eric Lindblad launched an expedition ship built for icy seas. Soon, small ships that had been strengthened to withstand ice shared the waters with private yachts, tall ships with canvas sails, and cruise ships. One of these floating cities carried 3,800 people, presenting a potential rescue nightmare. Last year, about 34,000 people sailed to Antarctica in 35 vessels, while smaller numbers arrived by air.

Most travelers converge on the Antarctic Peninsula, the popular tourist destination of the continent. They arrive during the Antarctic summer when seals and large colonies of penguins and seabirds raise their young onshore.

Since the M/S *Explorer* disaster in 2007, accidents have become common. From 2008 to 2011, ships struck rocks or ran aground every year. Many ships burn cheap, heavy fuel that pollutes the air and adds to global warming. All harm the habitat.

Tourists come right up to a colony of Chinstrap penguins on Half Moon Island off Antarctica. The black line around the penguins' white faces looks like a strap holding on a black helmet.

THE HUMAN IMPACT

Growing numbers of tourists who come ashore on small boats—even helicopters—have increased the concern for wildlife. Several years ago, biologist Steve Forrest, who worked on an island near the peninsula, said, "Some days we may see 600 people here." One British traveler observed tourists climbing into penguin colonies, and even chasing penguins, to get the perfect photo. Researchers are still learning whether such pressure disrupts colonies of breeding birds and seals. Other tourists have trampled delicate moss beds, which take a century to grow a few inches.

Scientists also worry about **invasive species**, which are non-native species that can take hold in a habitat and wipe out local plants and animals. Already, spiders, seeds, fruit flies, and human bacteria have hitchhiked here on boots, jackets, and backpacks. Global warming has increased temperatures in Antarctica, and many fear that invasive species, once kept out by the bitter cold, could begin thriving here.

Over 250,000 king penguins live in this colony on South Georgia Island off the Antarctica mainland.

The hitchhiker seeds caught on this hiker's boots show how invasive species are brought in.

WHO'S IN CHARGE?

Today, no one owns Antarctica, so no government enforces rules. Instead, the Antarctic Treaty, signed by 50 countries, protects Antarctica as "a natural reserve devoted to peace and science." Member countries solve legal problems themselves, and tourists obey the laws of their own countries.

To help protect the environment, the International Association of Antarctica Tour Operators (IAATO) developed strict conservation guidelines for its members. Tourists and guides must inspect their gear for invasive species and disinfect their boots before going ashore. Tourists who watch wildlife must keep their distance, be quiet, and respect nests and young wildlife. Recently, the Antarctic Treaty ruled that ships with 500-plus people cannot land in Antarctica. Smaller ships may visit a site one at a time but must limit landings to groups of 100. Guides must supervise every 20 people.

DO THE RULES WORK?

So far, self-regulation has prevented a catastrophe, but many worries linger. Not all tour companies belong to IAATO, and many yacht owners aren't aware of the rules.

Despite the rise in tourism, conservation work continues. In 2011, a United Nations (UN) agency banned cruise ships from using heavy fuel, a dangerous pollutant if spilled. As a result, three megaships cancelled tours for 2011/12, reducing tourist numbers by 9,000. The same UN agency hoped to release a Polar Code governing all tourism in 2012.

The Polar Code cannot go into effect soon enough. Already, adventure travelers come here to ski, snowboard, mountain climb, scuba, and kayak, and others ride motorbikes and skydive. Runners compete in marathons near the South Pole.

"Antarctica is like this giant world park," notes biologist Steve Forrest. "And we don't have any park rangers."

Explore the Issue

1. **Analyze Causes** How do tourists threaten habitats in Antarctica?

2. **Compare and Contrast** What are the benefits and drawbacks of keeping Antarctica accessible to tourists?

Saving Big Cats

Lion families in Kenya face extinction if their habitats are not saved. Healthy lionesses usually have litters of two to four cubs every two years.

GOING, GOING . . .

Think about this cold, hard fact. In 1960, 450,000 lions roamed the savannas of Africa, but today, only 20,000 of these magnificent creatures are left. In a mere 50 years, more than 90 percent of Africa's lions have been lost, most of them due to habitat destruction, poaching, sport hunting, and conflicts with people.

These statistics alarmed conservationists and filmmakers

Beverly and Dereck Joubert film wildlife in Africa.

Beverly and Dereck Joubert (joo-BEHR), National Geographic Explorers-in-Residence. For nearly 30 years, the Jouberts have filmed wildlife in the bush of Africa, and each of their 22 films delivers a forceful conservation message.

As the Jouberts learned, other big cats also teeter on the brink of extinction. Wild leopards have dwindled from 750,000 to 50,000, while cheetahs are down from 45,000 to 12,000. The case of tigers is the most shocking of all: only 3,000 still remain in the wild.

"We are seeing the effects of 7 billion people on the planet," Dereck says. "At present rates, we will lose the big cats in 10 to 15 years."

TIME FOR ACTION

To the Jouberts, these numbers signaled an impending disaster. Habitats need predators, such as lions, because they control populations of prey, which are animals the predators eat. Otherwise, too many prey animals strip away vegetation until the animals die from sickness and starvation. Then habitats crash along with communities that need them.

"We no longer have the luxury of time when it comes to big cats," says Dereck. "They are in such a downward spiral that if we hesitate now, we will be responsible for extinctions across the globe. If there was ever a time to take action, it is now." Therefore, in 2009, the Jouberts teamed with National Geographic to organize a bold **initiative**, or plan of action.

At work, the Jouberts film and photograph a leopard in its habitat.

"We no longer have the luxury of time when it comes to big cats." —Dereck Joubert

ROARING BACK

The Jouberts and National Geographic took action to create the Big Cats Initiative (BCI), an emergency fund. It supports fast-action projects to stop the decline of African lions by 2015 and then build numbers to healthy levels by 2020. So far, BCI has sponsored 21 projects in 13 countries. To help fund the BCI, the Jouberts filmed a documentary and have appeared on television news programs. Their appeal for funding to help prevent the downward spiral of the big cats is international.

The Jouberts face significant monetary, land, and attitudinal challenges. Protecting habitats takes millions of dollars, land for lions, and a global army of supporters. Through the Big Cats Initiative, the Jouberts have hope. Big cats multiply quickly if they are left undisturbed, and BCI's projects in Africa indicate a recovery could happen.

Another challenge the Jouberts face is changing the attitudes of people who live near lions. Lions need a huge habitat for hunting and having families. As the African human population grows, agricultural land is taken from the lions' habitat. When hungry lions come looking for prey on farms, villagers kill them to protect themselves and their livestock.

To protect big cats from human predators, BCI tests many ideas with local people. In Tanzania, project leaders show popular films explaining the benefits of lions and ways to coexist. Elsewhere, "living walls" reinforce wildlife pens with chain-link fences and fast-growing trees to protect people's cattle from lions. In return, people leave the lions alone. The initiative is showing results in Kenya, where herdsmen are repaid if lions kill their cattle. In a hopeful sign, fewer lions are being lost.

Population pressures remain a threat, but Dereck Joubert has begun to see possibilities. "It really depends on what those 7 billion people do. . . . We can build a real army of people fighting for conservation," he says.

Explore the Issue

1. **Analyze Cause and Effect** What human activities have affected the big cats? What is the effect of those activities?

2. **Identify Problems and Solutions** How has the Big Cats Initiative helped to preserve habitats?

Restore a Habitat
—and document your efforts

One strategy for inspiring people to do their part in protecting and preserving habitats is to shine a light on a problem they might not know about. You don't have to be a famous filmmaker to create an informative, engaging documentary. Showing how ordinary people can help encourages others to join in.

IDENTIFY

- Invite an expert from a local nature center, zoo, estuary, or botanical park to speak to your class. Learn about ways this organization protects and preserves habitats.

- Ask the expert about biodiversity in your area and habitats that are threatened.

- Find out how your group can help. With the expert, identify a center or an organization that could use your help for a day.

ORGANIZE

- Plan a class field trip to your identified location. Coordinate with the organization to figure out what work you will be performing and what you will need to bring.

- Before arriving, decide how you will document your class's efforts and work for the day.

- Collect notebooks, cameras, and video recorders to use while volunteering.

Students in Alabama plant dune grasses to help restore the coastal habitat.

DOCUMENT

- Interview people who work at the location and interview fellow students as you work on your volunteer project.

- Photograph the habitat. Record details about animals and birds, plants, water sources, and current threats.

- Create a multimedia documentary about the location and the work the class performed. Or, create a poster of a series of 10–12 photos with detailed captions.

SHARE

- Premiere your documentary at the location where you volunteered. Offer to have a "live showing" on a particular day and invite students' families to participate.

- Present your documentary to other classes and/or other grades at your school.

- Offer to write a short article for the school paper about your efforts.

Write an Argumentative Article

The Amazon rain forest is one of the largest and most biodiverse habitats on Earth, but today, rampant deforestation seriously threatens its future and ours. Write an article about the dangers facing the Amazon rain forest and what individuals should do to save it. Focus on a specific solution that ordinary people should adopt to conserve this dwindling rain forest.

RESEARCH

Use the Internet, books, and articles to answer these questions:

- What dangers threaten the Amazon rain forest? What are the major, strongly held viewpoints about its use?
- What agricultural, consumer, and business practices endanger its future? What can or should be done about those practices?
- What is your viewpoint and proposed solution after your research?

Your research is the backbone of your argument. Be sure to take notes, record your sources, and find statistics or quotations to support your viewpoint.

DRAFT

Review your notes and then write a first draft.

- The first paragraph, or introduction, should clearly introduce your claim and present the problem. State your argument and what you think should be done and then organize your reasons and evidence clearly.
- In the second paragraph, or body, identify the threats to the rain forest that you pinpoint in your argument. Use clear reasons and relevant evidence, such as statistics or quotations from your notes, to support your claim. Make sure you use credible sources for your data.
- In the third paragraph, or conclusion, write a concluding statement arguing for choices that you want consumers or individuals to make to protect rain forests. Emphasize the importance of your argument.

REVISE & EDIT

Read your first draft to make sure it presents a strong case for making choices that protect the rain forest.

- Does your introduction clearly state your claim? Do you introduce your argument and support your claim with clear reasons and relevant evidence?
- Does the body clearly explain activities that harm the rain forest and show how your suggestions for improvement will help further conservation?
- In your conclusion, have you persuaded readers to make specific changes to preserve the rain forest?

Revise your article to make sure it covers all the bases. Then proofread your paper for errors in spelling and punctuation. Are names spelled correctly and are quotations accurate? Be sure your argument presents evidence logically and links problems to solutions.

PUBLISH & PRESENT

Now you are ready to publish and present your argument. Add any images or graphs, and then print out or write a clean copy by hand. Post your article in the classroom and discuss your ideas with classmates.

Visual GLOSSARY

habitat

invasive species

biodiversity *n.*, the variety of living things on Earth

conservation *n.*, the work of preserving habitats and living things

deforestation *n.*, the removal of trees in a forest to convert the land for farming or other uses

extinct *adj.*, describing a species that no longer exists

habitat *n.*, the natural home of a living thing, providing food, water, and shelter

initiative *n.*, a plan of action

invasive species *n.*, a nonnative species that invades a habitat and may destroy native plants and animals

overconsumption *n.*, the use of natural resources faster than they can be replaced

peninsula *n.*, a narrow strip of land projecting from the mainland into a sea or a lake

primate *n.*, an order of mammal that includes lemurs, monkeys, apes, and humans

slash-and-burn agriculture *n.*, the cutting and burning of forests to open fields for farming or pastures

species *n.*, kinds of living things with similar features that can interbreed

urban sprawl *n.*, the spread of cities into surrounding land

primate

slash-and-burn agriculture

deforestation

INDEX

SKILLS